SCOTTISH BUSES

A Colour Portfolio

Gavin Booth

Ian Allan
PUBLISHING

Introduction

It was exciting to be living and working in Scotland in the 1980s. The bus industry had enjoyed half a century of regulated stability, and there was a mixture of trepidation and excitement about the changes that the 1980s would bring. I was working with Scottish Bus Group as the group's marketing manager for most of the decade, and was heavily involved in express coach deregulation, the Scotmap market-research exercise, the creation of Scottish Citylink, the 1985 reorganisation of the group in anticipation of bus-service deregulation, and the infamous Glasgow 'bus wars'. All of these events are covered in the book, along with the more mundane everyday bus services that played — and still play — such an important part in the country's economy.

Scotland is not all castles and seascapes like the cover photograph, and I have tried to reflect the sheer variety of operating conditions, from the glamour of shiny new express coaches to the grim realities of urban bus operation. The photos are all my own, taken in Scotland during the 1980s. One of the advantages of my role at SBG was the opportunity to travel around Scotland and see at first hand what was happening. And, enthusiast to the last, I didn't always point my camera at SBG vehicles. I need hardly add that non-SBG buses were always photographed in my own time…

The 1980s in Scotland, as in the rest of Britain, was a decade of unprecedented change. The safe and — whisper it — comfortable years of regulation and monopoly were fast drawing to a close in the face of Nicholas Ridley's interpretation of Thatcherism. The first rumblings had come with the announcement that express coach services would be deregulated in 1980, bringing to an end 50 years of regulation and licensing that looked after the interests of the operators (if not necessarily the customers). And, the industry surmised, bus deregulation could not be far behind. It wasn't.

From 1985 the bus industry in Britain outside London was in a state of suspended animation, and from 1986 the reality bit, as hitherto-sacred monopolies were breached by entrepreneurial upstarts. And, although the Scottish Bus Group escaped privatisation in the 1980s (if only just), the building-blocks were in place for the most fundamental changes to the ownership of the country's buses in over half a century.

For these reasons the 1980s must, in football terms, be regarded as a decade of two halves, and the photographs in this book are divided in this way — the first part dealing with the uneasy calm of the period between 1980 and 1984 and the second part covering the amazing and unparalleled changes that took place between 1985 and 1989.

The Scottish bus industry in 1980 was dominated by two groups of operators. The Scottish Bus Group, operating through seven companies, ran 3,800 buses on rural, urban and inter-urban services over much of the mainland and on some of the West Coast islands. The other major group consisted of the four former municipal fleets, now under PTE (Strathclyde) or

Front cover: The picture-postcard image of Scotland — a castle, the sea and distant hills — is captured in this 1985 view of an Arran Coaches 1975 Bedford YRQ with 45-seat Plaxton Derwent body leaving Lochranza on the island of Arran in May 1985 against the backdrop of Lochranza Castle, Kilbrannan Sound and the hills of the Kintyre peninsula.

Previous page: Delays in the delivery of Alexander bodies prompted Eastern Scottish to turn to Plaxton in 1978 — the first time SBG had bought new Plaxton bodies. ZS961D, a 1980 Seddon Pennine VII with Supreme IV bodywork, sits at South Queensferry in September 1981 on a coach tour, against the always dramatic backdrop of the Forth Bridge. In Eastern's fleet numbering system, the 'Z' prefix denoted a dual-purpose vehicle while the 'D' suffix indicates that it was allocated to Galashiels depot.

First published 2003

ISBN 0 7110 2951 2

Published by Ian Allan Publishing

an imprint of Ian Allan Publishing Ltd, Hersham, Surrey KT12 4RG.
Printed by Ian Allan Printing Ltd, Hersham, Surrey KT12 4RG.

Code: 0304/B2

Regional (Grampian, Lothian, Tayside) control; between them they added a further 2,100 buses to the total.

Many of Scotland's best-known independent operators had disappeared by 1980, some following acquisition by SBG companies, but well-known names that were still active included the Ayrshire co-operatives AA, A1 and Clyde Coast, two of the Paisley-area fleets — Graham's and McGill's — and, elsewhere in west central Scotland, Garelochhead Coach Services and Hutchison of Overtown. Then there were two growing Fife independents — Moffat & Williamson and Rennie's — and, in the Perth area, McLennan of Spittalfield. Further north, Newton's of Dingwall had built up a sizeable fleet, much of it used on contract services in connection with the burgeoning North Sea oil business. Prominent Scottish coaching companies were Cotter's Tours, Dodds of Troon and Park's of Hamilton.

In the early 1980s there was much activity on the express-coaching front as operators took advantage of their new-found freedom. One of the first was Perth-based Gloagtrotter, which started a Glasgow–London overnight service on 9 October 1980 at fares that undercut the well-established Western SMT service. 'Gloagtrotter' would soon be replaced by the more familiar Stagecoach name. Also dabbling in express services was Park's, which joined the British Coachways consortium and operated between Edinburgh/Glasgow and London. Cotter's Tours launched a more upmarket product in December 1980 — its Coachline service between Edinburgh/Glasgow and London, with Volvo/ Van Hool coaches featuring video films and on-board catering. The Scottish Bus Group companies fought back with new coaches and reduced fares and in 1983 created Scottish Citylink to pull together its separately-branded express-coaching operation.

The other fight at this time involved Strathclyde PTE and the monopoly boundary imposed in 1930 to protect Glasgow's municipal tramcars. Fifty years later this was still in place, which meant that longer-distance SBG services could not pick up and set down the same passengers within the boundary area. From August 1982 the boundary conditions were abolished, and SBG vehicles were able to provide a more comprehensive service on the corridors they used. After deregulation it would become academic anyway.

SBG embarked on a massive market-research programme — Scotmap — in 1980, and this resulted in substantial service revisions over the next few years, as well as a move to increase the number of double-deckers in the fleet. In 1984 SBG announced major changes to the structure of the group, creating four new bus companies by rearranging operational boundaries, in anticipation of bus-service deregulation.

Deregulation duly came in October 1986 — a few weeks earlier in Glasgow, by agreement between Strathclyde PTE, the operators and the Traffic Commissioners. SBG companies moved into urban networks in Scotland's four main cities — Aberdeen, Dundee, Edinburgh and (most notoriously) Glasgow, where the extra buses on the city streets caused massive congestion. At the same time, the four local-authority fleets also took advantage of deregulation by moving out beyond their traditional boundaries, while existing independents introduced new services. There were newcomers too, notably Stagecoach, operating as Magic Bus in Glasgow using former London Routemasters; the Routemaster was a feature of Scottish deregulation, as three of the new SBG fleets — Clydeside, Kelvin and Strathtay — saw their potential as fast and manoeuvrable buses in the competitive arena.

By the end of the 1980s the Scottish bus industry faced further uncertainties, particularly regarding ownership. The privatisation of the National Bus Company in England and Wales had taken place between 1986 and 1988, and, although SBG hoped it might escape the sell-off, plans to privatise the group were announced in 1988; the actual sales did not begin until 1990. Local authorities were also encouraged to sell off their bus fleets, and Grampian Regional Transport was the first in Scotland to be sold, for £5 million in a management-led employee buy-out — a first small step in a process that would lead to the creation of today's FirstGroup.

By 1990 the fleets of the big Scottish operators had reduced quite dramatically. The nine bus-operating SBG companies fielded just over 3,000 vehicles, and the local-authority fleets (including now-privatised Grampian) just 1,700 — an overall drop of over 20% in the size of the 'public' fleets. Several well-known independent names had disappeared, some had come and gone during the decade, and others had grown, partly on the back of deregulation. Two once-prominent independents disappeared in the 1980s: Garelochhead Coach Services ceased trading in 1980 and McLennan of Spittalfield was taken over by Stagecoach in 1985.

As the decade ended, the Scottish bus industry was waiting with some trepidation to see what would happen in the SBG sell-off. The politicians said they hoped to see employee buy-outs, and, while this did indeed happen, there was the fear that some of the more aggressive new groups, born out of NBC deregulation, would have their sights set on Scotland. The shape of the bus business north of the border was about to change for ever...

Gavin Booth
Edinburgh
November 2002

3

Above: The brave new world of deregulated express coaching represented by the British Coachways consortium reached Edinburgh one cold December day in 1980. At the Frederick Street terminal point on the very first departure from the city is a Volvo B58/Plaxton Supreme of Park's of Hamilton with, it would appear, just one passenger. The Edinburgh–London coach fed into the Glasgow–London service at Hamilton. Park's never painted any of its coaches in British Coachways livery and continued the services after the consortium's collapse in October 1982.

Right: Central SMT, probably the most traditional of the seven Scottish Bus Group companies, broke new ground in 1981 when it introduced a new cross-Glasgow service linking East Kilbride in the south with Clydebank across the River Clyde and to the west, in spite of opposition from Strathclyde PTE. It used new Dennis Dominators with 79-seat Alexander RL-type bodies; D2 is seen at East Kilbride in September 1981.

Above: The Dennis Dorchester was introduced in 1983 as a Gardner-mid-engined heavyweight chassis to rival the Leyland Tiger and Seddon Pennine VII. SBG's Central and Western companies took Dorchesters; this is Central's DD8, one of five with 49-seat Alexander TE-type bodywork delivered in 1984, in East Kilbride when new.

Right: Bedfords and Fords were bought by several SBG companies in the 1970s, ostensibly for lighter rural duties. Alexander (Midland) MT36, a 1975 R1014 with 45-seat Alexander AYS-type body, is seen in April 1981 at the fine Gleneagles railway station built to serve the five-star hotel of the same name, on the service to nearby Auchterarder.

Left: The Fleetline was SBG's main choice for rear-engined double-deckers in the 1960s and '70s. Western SMT MR75, a 1980 Leyland Fleetline FE30AGR with 75-seat Alexander AD-type body, turns from Argyle Street, Glasgow into Jamaica Street in August 1984. In Western's fleet-numbering system, recently re-started at 1 after reaching 2984, the letter 'M' is the depot code (Thornliebank, but 'M' for historical reasons) and the 'R' represents the last letter of Daimler; the fact that it was called a Leyland would not cause Western to change its code.

Above: This new version of Western SMT's black-and-white coaching livery was introduced in 1980 and is seen here in May 1982 at Rothesay Pier on the island of Bute on RS2648, a 1977 Seddon Pennine VII with 49-seat Alexander AT-type bodywork. The Pennine VII was developed for SBG as a Gardner-engined equivalent to the Leyland Leopard and was bought by Eastern Scottish and Western SMT.

Left: Heading through Cullen in September 1984, an Alexander (Northern) Leyland Leopard PSU3/3R with 49-seat Alexander AY-type bodywork. New to Western SMT in 1973, it was transferred north in 1983 to become NPE130; the 'A' suffix to the fleetnumber denotes its home depot, Aberdeen. Inter-company transfers were a regular happening in SBG, as the more profitable fleets in central Scotland cascaded buses to the more marginal companies. In some cases these transfers resulted from dissatisfaction with a particular type of bus, but the Leopard was a popular workhorse throughout the group.

Above: Alexander (Northern) NPE103, a 1980 Leyland Leopard PSU3F/4R with 49-seat Alexander AT-type body, brightens up a wet April afternoon in the centre of Banff on the long service to Aberdeen. The 'MF' suffix to the fleetnumber indicates that it is based at nearby Macduff depot.

Left: SBG's famous Bristol REMH6G/Alexander M-type coaches were a familiar sight on Scotland–London express services for many years. Later in its life, in May 1982, Alexander (Northern) NE1, an ex-Western SMT 1971 example, sits in Dundee bus station in the later version of the blue/white Scottish corporate livery introduced with the first Leyland Tigers for the group.

Above: After years of receiving a mix of lightweight Fords and cast-offs from other SBG fleets, from the late 1970s Highland Omnibuses received new heavyweight buses, and from 1980 it took delivery of 18 Leyland National 2 NL116L11/1R models for urban work. N7, a 1980 52-seater, is seen in Academy Street, Inverness, on a town service in May 1984.

Right: Highland also received six new Leyland Olympians, in 1983, with 77-seat Alexander RL-type bodies. The first of these, J1, is seen in Academy Street, Inverness, on the same day in May 1984 as the National in the previous photograph.

Left: Strathclyde PTE had a bit of an identity crisis in the early 1980s until it settled on a new fleetname to replace the 'GG' symbol it had used when it was Greater Glasgow PTE. In Clarkston in August 1983 is LO40, a newly-delivered Leyland Olympian ONTL11/1R with low-height 78-seat ECW bodywork. It wears the not unattractive green/yellow/black livery with Trans-Clyde fleetnames, introduced in 1980. After receiving its last Leyland Atlanteans, in 1981, SPTE bought Olympians and MCW Metrobuses before purchasing a sizeable batch of Volvo-Ailsas.

Above: Cooling problems at St Enoch Square terminus in Glasgow city centre on a hot August day in 1983. The inspector prepares to top up the water level on A62, a 1982 Volvo-Ailsa B55-10 with 79-seat Alexander RV-type bodywork. The 'U' symbol is for the adjacent Underground station.

Above: In 1983 SPTE adopted yet another livery — the so-called
'Strathclyde Red' seen on 1977 Leyland Atlantean AN68A/1R
No LA1204, with 78-seat Alexander AL-type body. It is in Union Street,
Glasgow, in August 1984, passing a contemporary, LA1188, in the 1980
livery.

Right: One of SPTE's very last Leyland Atlanteans, LA1440 of 1981,
with Alexander 66-seat body, is seen in Summerston in August 1984.
It wears full SPTE orange livery with Strathclyde Transport fleetnames.
The side advert explains the low seating capacity, as it is one of four
rebuilt in 1983 to carry up to three wheelchairs on the lower deck,
with access through the door behind the front axle.

Left: GGPTE bought a trial batch of five early MCW Metrobuses in 1979; later Metrobuses for the fleet would have Alexander bodies, but the first five had 77-seat MCW bodies, as on MB2 in Renfield Street, Glasgow, in August 1983.

Above: Neither GGPTE nor its predecessor, Glasgow Corporation, had ever operated large numbers of single-deckers, but in 1979 the PTE bought 20 Leyland National 10351A/1R 41-seaters. LN15 is in George Square, Glasgow, in August 1983.

Above: Lothian Region Transport continued Edinburgh Corporation's practice of buying Alexander-bodied Leyland Atlanteans. No 807, a 1966 Corporation-bought PDR1/1 with 74-seat A-type body, is seen at Greenbank in April 1981; it was one of the only batch of short-windowed Atlanteans bought for Edinburgh, as all subsequent examples had panoramic side windows.

Right: Two Lothian Leyland Atlantean PDR1A/1 with dual-door 75-seat Alexander J-type bodies pick up passengers at The Mound, Edinburgh, in September 1983. No 364 was new in 1970. It will be noted that the panoramic windows did not line up on the offside of these buses.

Above: Tayside Regional Council standardised on Volvo-Ailsa double-deckers but also tried an (unsuccessful) batch of Bristol VRTs, as well as an MCW Metrobus and a small batch of Dennis Dominators. Long-wheelbase Dominator No 284 of 1981, with East Lancs 79-seat dual-door body, is seen in the centre of Dundee in May 1982.

Right: Grampian Regional Transport continued Aberdeen Corporation's vehicle-buying policy with a substantial fleet of Alexander-bodied Leyland Atlanteans delivered between 1976 and 1983. New in 1980, No 297, an AN68A/1R with 74-seat dual-door AL-type body, is in Union Street, Aberdeen, in June 1981. The vehicles that follow are not evidence of the legendary thrift of Aberdonians but cars taking part in a rally.

Left: Irvine Cross was always a popular place to catch the buses of the two most famous Ayrshire co-operatives, AA Buses and A1 Service. At the cross in April 1983 A1 Service OCS 345L, a 1972 Leyland Atlantean AN68/2R with Leeds-style Roe body, passes AA's first Leyland National, a 1972 1151/1R 52-seater. The Atlantean was owned by Docherty of Irvine, and the National by Young of Ayr. Although buses in similar liveries can still be seen at this point today, they are owned by Stagecoach Western Buses.

Above: A later AA National, a 1981 National 2 NL116AL11/1R 52-seater, approaches Irvine Cross from the east, showing signs of a temporary window repair. It was owned by Dodds of Troon.

Left: Representing the fleet of McLennan, Spittalfield, one of the first companies to be acquired by Stagecoach, is preserved Daimler CCG5 TFA 987, new to Burton-on-Trent Corporation in 1964 with Massey bodywork. It is seen at Caputh in September 1984. McLennan's Perth–Errol service was acquired by Stagecoach in December 1980, and founder Brian Souter took his PSV test in a similar bus from the fleet.

Above: Rather unexpectedly, Alexander (Midland) painted this 1980 Leyland Leopard PSU3E/4R, MPE371, in National Holidays livery to work coaching holidays for the English firm. It has Duple Dominant II 49-seat body and is seen outside Midland's Perth depot in September 1984.

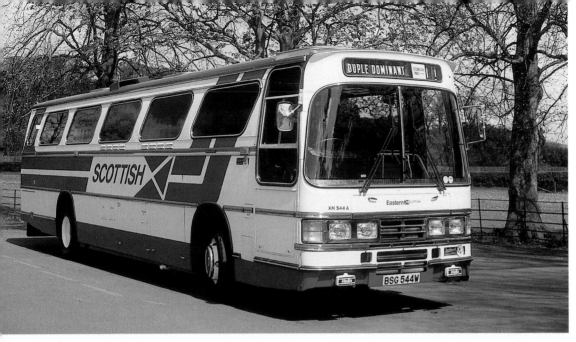

Left: A famous coach — the Eastern Scottish prototype Leyland B43 (Tiger) XH544A, with Duple Dominant III 46-seat bodywork. It was one of the Tigers taken to Morocco for the spectacular launch of that model in 1981. A TRCTL11/3R model, it is seen at Dryburgh Abbey Hotel in the Borders — owned by SBG — in May 1981. The 'X' prefix indicates a toilet-fitted coach, while the 'A' suffix denotes allocation to New Street, Edinburgh.

Right: Another famous SBG vehicle — the prototype MCW Metroliner double-deck coach, launched at the 1982 Motor Show. It was used by Western SMT on the Glasgow–London service from April 1983, when it was photographed at Buchanan Bus Station after arriving on its maiden trip from London. The blue/yellow livery anticipated the scheme chosen for Scottish Citylink, launched later that year. Originally a demonstrator, TSX 1Y was bought by Alexander (Northern) in 1984.

Left: SBG's answer to National Express, Scottish Citylink, was launched on 1 October 1983, using specially-liveried coaches from group fleets. On that first day Western SMT V541, a 1975 Volvo B58 with Alexander M-type body, is seen at Buchanan Bus Station, Glasgow, on the frequent Glasgow–Edinburgh Express service, complete with typical SBG window stickers. The T-type at its side is in an advertising livery for Glasgow Airport.

Left: McGill's of Barrhead, the long-established Paisley-area independent, upset the *status quo* with a new service introduced in April 1983 linking Auchenback and the centre of Glasgow, often using two rare articulated Leyland-DAB buses with Roe-built bodies incorporating Leyland National parts. Still carrying the fleetnumber allocated by its original owner, South Yorkshire PTE, FHE 292V stands in Glasgow at Park's City Coach Station in the shadow of the Scottish Transport Group's Buchanan Bus Station in August 1983.

Above: Park's of Hamilton bought a large fleet of Volvo B10Ms with Duple Goldliner III bodies in 1982 and had ordered two articulated versions that never materialised following the banning of such coaches from the third lane of motorways. FHS 726X is seen ready for loading at Park's City Coach Station in Glasgow in June 1982.

Left: Although Cotter's became well-known for its Scotland–London Coachline services, it was primarily a tour operator. A Cotter's Tours Volvo B10M with Van Hool Alizée body — an early example of a combination that would be popular throughout the UK for some 20 years — is seen leaving the Caledonian MacBrayne car ferry at Craignure, on the island of Mull, in May 1985. The Cotter's business closed in 1987, with Wallace Arnold taking over the coach tours and Stagecoach the Coachline service.

Right: Allander Travel, Milngavie, was another Scottish coaching firm that grasped the opportunities offered by express deregulation and with Newton's of Dingwall started joint services between Edinburgh/Glasgow and Inverness. Loading in Strothers Lane, near Inverness bus station, in April 1982 is FHS 768X, a Volvo B10M with Duple Dominant IV bodywork.

Above: Stagecoach rose to prominence during the 1980s as it took full advantage of the opportunities presented by express and bus deregulation and the NBC privatisation. In an early version of the classic Stagecoach 'stripey' livery, two Bristol Lodekkas stand at the Perth Harbour premises it used as a depot before moving to Walnut Grove on the fringe of the same city. Both buses were among the very first double-deckers bought by the fledgling company — 866 NHT was one of two convertible-open-top FS6Gs bought from Bristol Omnibus Co, and HGM 335E was a former Central SMT extra-long FLF6G.

Right: Stagecoach quickly moved on to more exotic double-deckers like these vehicles parked in Regent Road, Edinburgh, in August 1983. The leading vehicles are 1982 75-seat Neoplan N122 Skyliners, a type favoured for a number of years on the upmarket Super Stage services; behind is one of three less successful 80-seat Van Hool Astromega coaches that lasted less than two years in the fleet.

Left: Scotland's native bus bodybuilder was Walter Alexander, which from the 1970s had built up a useful export business, supplying bodywork in kit and built-up form. In the finishing shop at the Falkirk coachworks in May 1980 are two Leyland Atlantean AN68/2L models for Metro Manila in the Philippines. These were from an order for 22 and were the first left-hand-drive bodies built by Alexander; the two buses shown were the only bodies from the order built at Falkirk, as the remainder were assembled in the Philippines from kits supplied.

Right: On the roads around Falkirk there is still a chance of seeing exotic machinery that has been built at the coachworks, now known as TransBus Falkirk. This three-axle Volvo-Ailsa B55 'Superjumbo' was spotted on test in Stenhousemuir in June 1981; it was one of two delivered later that year to China Motor Bus, Hong Kong, with 11.84m-long 101-seat RX-type bodies.

Above: A symbol of the new order, post-deregulation — London Buses' RM652 in Argyle Street, Glasgow in August 1985 working for the newly-created Clydeside Scottish company, complete with a full set of blinds. It was the first of what grew to be a substantial Routemaster fleet at Clydeside and would later be given the name *Rodney the Routemaster*.

Right: Still in Western SMT livery but with newly-applied Clydeside Scottish fleetnames and SBG's 'Best Bus' vinyls, J86, a 1980 Leyland Fleetline FE30AGR with 75-seat Alexander AD-type body in Gauze Street, Paisley, in July 1985.

Left: Clydeside adopted a striking red/yellow livery, here lacking company fleetnames but with the 'Welcome aboard. We're going your way.' vinyls Clydeside applied. The bus is ex-Western M174, a 1979 Leyland Fleetline FE30AGR with 75-seat Northern Counties bodywork, which has been adapted with a 'HELP' bumper and an electronic blind display. It is seen at Buchanan Bus Station, Glasgow, in October 1986.

Above: Photographed at Carstairs Village in April 1989 on an Omnibus Society Scottish Branch tour, Clydeside SRMA1, named 'George the Routemaster' after Clydeside General Manager George Watson, who introduced the type to SBG. It is a 1966 forward-entrance Routemaster used initially on BEA services and acquired from London Buses. It wears Clydeside's Quicksilver express livery.

41

Left: The original livery chosen for Kelvin Scottish was this restrained match of pale blue with Midland blue, but the management soon opted for a more dramatic yellow/blue scheme. At Cumbernauld depot in May 1985, ready for the launch of the new companies, is the bus that would shortly become Kelvin's M29, a 1982 MCW Metrobus with 78-seat Alexander RL-type body, alongside similar MRM58, of 1983, still in Midland colours.

Below left: The 'honour' of operating SBG's first new-generation minibus went to Kelvin Scottish, which bought 43 of these Mercedes-Benz L608Ds with 21-seat Alexander AM-type bodies in 1986. One of the first, No 1103, is seen outside Buchanan Bus Station, Glasgow, shortly after delivery in July 1986. It carries the yellow/blue livery recently adopted by Kelvin.

Right: Kelvin reversed its colours on a batch of 10 MCW Metrobuses with 78-seat Alexander RL-type bodywork bought for Cumbernauld express services in 1986. No 2677 is seen crossing Argyle Street in October 1986.

Above: Lowland Scottish, operating in the Borders, chose a light green/yellow livery but quickly opted for a darker green. In the original colours, No 172, a 1977 Leyland National 11351A/1R 52-seater, stands outside the company's main depot at Galashiels; the company head office was also on this site. The bus is from SBG's first batch of Leyland Nationals, bought to counteract vehicle shortages at Eastern Scottish, and inherited by Lowland from that fleet in 1985.

Right: Lowland's darker green livery is shown on this former Eastern Scottish Daimler Fleetline CRG6LXB with 75-seat ECW body, No 835, seen in the centre of Galashiels in April 1987.

Above: Variety in the Lowland fleet in April 1987. In Galashiels depot are, from right, No 714, a new Bedford VAS5 with 17-seat Reeve-Burgess body for the Border Courier service; No 543, a 1985 Leyland Tiger TRCTL11/2RH with Plaxton Paramount 3200 49-seat body; and, in Scottish Citylink colours, No 501, a 1987 Tiger TRCTL11/3RH with Paramount 3200 50-seat body. The Border Courier was an innovative service involving Lowland, Borders Regional Council and the local health board, combining passenger services in deep rural areas with the collection and delivery of medical supplies.

Right: In addition to the Fleetlines and Olympians passed on from Eastern Scottish, Lowland acquired former Central Dennis Dominators, including this Alexander AL-bodied example, previously Central D2, and seen in its original form on page 5. It is seen as Lowland No 655 in September 1988.

Above: My first sight of the new Strathtay Scottish livery was in April 1985 in Dundee depot. Shortly to be numbered SO7, this Leyland Olympian ONLXB/1R with 77-seat ECW body had been new to Northern Scottish in 1982. The blue/marigold livery was later adapted with the use of white relief.

Right: Strathtay inherited some of the last Alexander Y-type bodies built on Leyland Leopard chassis for SBG companies. SL43, a PSU3G/4R with 53-seat AYS-type body, is seen in Dundee High Street in October 1987, with a Routemaster in pursuit. New to Northern Scottish in 1982, this is a significant vehicle as it was the last Y-type Leopard for the Bus Group and, indeed, the last to be built.

Left: Strathtay also bought Routemasters from London. Although they initially operated in fleet colours, some were allocated to Perth and painted in this red/cream Perth City Transport livery, to compete with the locally-based Stagecoach. No SR6, formerly RM1821, turns into Scott Street, Perth, in 1989.

Above: Another competitive livery adopted by Strathtay was that of the fictional Mackay's Coaches, which was introduced to deal with competition from Smith, Coupar Angus, on the Perth–Blairgowrie route. The 'Mackay's' coach is really Strathtay SL20, a 1977 Leyland Leopard PSU3E/4R with 49-seat Duple Dominant I body, and is seen in Perth in March 1989 with a Smith coach behind.

Left: Eastern Scottish also got involved in imitating an independent when it painted the 1978 Seddon Pennine VII/ Alexander AYS-type 53-seater on the right in colours similar to those of Harris, Armadale, competing on the Armadale–Bathgate–Blackburn–Whitburn route with its ex-Northern Scottish 1978 Ford R1114 with similar bodywork. Eastern's independent imitation went as far as non-uniformed driver and crude destination information. The buses are seen in Bathgate in August 1988.

Above: While other SBG fleets were buying second-hand Routemasters from London to stock their fleets in the face of possible competition, Eastern Scottish turned to South Yorkshire PTE for Volvo-Ailsas with 75-seat Van Hool-McArdle bodies. VV6, new in 1976, is seen in Princes Street, Edinburgh, in March 1988.

Above: SBG dabbled in double-deck coaches in the 1980s, including two of these Leyland Olympian ONTL11/1R with unique low-height Alexander RDC 63-seat bodies. Initially in a blue/yellow livery, by 1989 they were in this green/cream Eastern Express scheme. No CLL144N, new in 1984, is seen in March 1989 at Bathgate. The 'C' prefix to the fleetnumber indicates, wrongly, that it is in Citylink colours; the 'N' suffix denotes allocation to Livingston depot.

Right: Midland Scottish lost its operations in the area around Glasgow to the new Kelvin Scottish company in June 1985. A month earlier, Leyland Leopard PSU3C/3R No MPE249, new in 1977, with 53-seat Alexander AY-type body, picks up passengers in the Kilsyth area.

Above: The most typical SBG minibus was the Dodge S56 with Alexander AM-type body, supplied to several group fleets in the 1980s. Fife Scottish FM1G, a 25-seat example of 1987, is seen in BuzzBus livery leaving Glenrothes bus station on a local service in October 1987.

Right: Turning out of Glenrothes bus station in October 1987 is Fife Scottish FRA108G, a 1985 Volvo Citybus B10M-50 with 80-seat Alexander bodywork. The registration number and non-SBG standard destination display reveals that this was not one of the Citybuses bought new by Fife but a former Volvo demonstrator, bought in 1987.

Above left: Walter Alexander's successor to the much-loved Y-type family was the P-type, a design that lacked the Y-type's flair. Northern Scottish NBT24A, a 1984 Leyland Tiger TRBLXB/2RH with 52-seat P-type body, descends Guild Street towards Aberdeen bus station in October 1987. The 'ugly duckling' P-type would re-emerge as the much more attractive PS, beloved of Stagecoach and Mainline. The Gardner option on the Tiger was introduced largely to satisfy SBG demand for such a combination, in the face of competition from models like the Seddon Pennine VII and Dennis Dorchester.

Left: Highland Scottish operated coaches in its own and Citylink liveries. In grey/blue at the Broadford airstrip on the Isle of Skye in October 1987 is E190S, a 1985 Leyland Tiger TRCTL11/3RH with 46-seat Duple Laser 2 bodywork.

Above: Western Scottish operated into Oban from its Ardrishaig depot until the June 1985 SBG reorganisation, when its operations in Ardrishaig and on the island of Islay passed to Midland; at the same time Midland regained its Oban area from Highland. In Oban in May 1985 is MS664, a Western Seddon Pennine VII with 49-seat Alexander AY-type bodywork; 'C7' above the fleetnumber indicates that it was new in 1977.

Above: In 1988 SBG's Clydeside company was reunited with Western. At the former Clydeside Greenock depot in October 1989 are three Western buses — from right a 1985 Dennis Dominator/Alexander RL-type in the current version of the company's livery, a 1983 Dennis Dorchester/Plaxton Paramount 3200 and a 1980 Leyland Leopard/ Alexander AY-type still in Clydeside colours.

Right: In 1988 Kelvin and Central were combined as Kelvin Central Buses. In simplified Kelvin livery is No 1943, the former London Routemaster RM367, in Argyle Street, Glasgow.

Left: The M8 motorway cuts through the centre of Glasgow. Crossing it at Woodlands Road, near Charing Cross, in July 1986, is Strathclyde PTE A75, a 1982 Volvo-Ailsa B55-10 Mk III with 79-seat Alexander RV-type body — a popular combination in Glasgow at the time.

Right: Lothian Region Transport belatedly turned to Leyland Nationals in 1982 and over the next three years accumulated a fleet of 20 National 2s. No 141, new in 1985, turns from Edinburgh's George Street into St Andrew Square. It is an NL116TL11/2R model with dual-door 45-seat body.

Left: After its Atlanteans, Lothian started building up a fleet of long-wheelbase Leyland Olympians — initially with ECW bodies, which caused political ructions in view of the change from locally-built Alexander bodywork. No 725, a 1983 ONTL11/2R with 83-seat dual-door ECW body, is seen in Princes Street in July 1986. Leyland was aggressively selling complete Olympians with bodies built in its own plants at ECW and Roe, and SBG and Strathclyde PTE also briefly turned to ECW bodywork at the same time.

Above: In the 1980s London Buses had 115 Leaside District MCW Metrobuses converted from hydraulic to air braking by SBG Engineering at its Marine Works in Edinburgh. Caught in Princes Street in 1987 is M1325, alongside a 1975 Lothian Atlantean.

Above: Grampian Transport introduced this attractive livery variation at the time of deregulation. At Marischal College in October 1986 is 1979 Leyland Atlantean AN68A/1R No 271 with 74-seat Alexander AL-type body.

Below left: Thirty Leyland Olympians were bought by Grampian between 1984 and 1988. From the 1984 batch, No 106, an ONLXB/1R with 73-seat dual-door Alexander RH-type body, is seen in Guild Street in October 1987.

Right: Unusual buses for Tayside Regional Council in 1984 were four of these short (9.5m) Leyland Tiger TRCTL11/1R models with 35-seat dual-purpose Reeve Burgess bodies. No 233, named *Strathmore*, is seen in Meadowside, Dundee, in March 1985.

Left: As the SBG companies prepared for privatisation, more non-group companies became involved in operating Scottish Citylink services. One of the more unusual coaches to wear the livery was this Dodds of Troon 1982 Volvo B10M with rare Italian-built Padane ZX coachwork, seen at Glasgow's Buchanan Bus Station in July 1988. Padane coachwork was first introduced into the UK in 1980; this was one of several similar coaches acquired by Dodds from Townsend-Thoresen in 1986.

Above: Silver Coach Lines of Edinburgh has operated some interesting coaches, including this little ACE Puma with Van Hool Alizée body, seen in Argyle Street, Glasgow, in June 1987. At the time, Silver Coach Lines was owned by the Walter Alexander coachbuilding business, but in 1989 there was a management buy-out and the company invested in a fleet of new Setras. ACE (Alternative Chassis Engineering) built small quantities of chassis in Huddersfield; the Puma had a DAF engine.

Left: Only 10 of Volvo's C10M coaches were sold to UK operators, and three from the Park's of Hamilton fleet are seen together in Regent Road, Edinburgh, in July 1988. The C10M was introduced to the UK in 1985, a premium coach built in Switzerland by Ramseier & Jenzer. A year later the C10M was deleted from Volvo's UK range.

Below left: Graham's Bus Service was one of the longer-surviving Paisley-area independents. In Gauze Street, Paisley, in August 1989 is S1, a 1977 Leyland Leopard PSU3D/4R with new 55-seat Plaxton Derwent body fitted in 1987.

Right: The mis-spelt destination says it all — a 1975 AEC Reliance 6MU4R with 45-seat Willowbrook body of Irvine of Salsburgh at the dismal Shotts terminus of its route to Airdrie.

Left: Clyde Coast Services was the smallest of the long-surviving Ayrshire co-operatives, whereby two or more operators ran jointly using a common livery and fleetname. WCS 831K, a 1972 Leyland Atlantean PDR1A/1 with 78-seat Alexander J-type body, is seen in Largs, with the Caledonian MacBrayne car ferry to Cumbrae Slip at the pier in the background. This Atlantean, owned by McGregor, Saltcoats, came from the best-known of the co-operatives, A1 Service.

Right: Royal Mail Post Buses provide combined passenger/mail services in Scotland's more deeply rural areas. Here at Dunoon in May 1985 is a 1983 Ford Transit with Dormobile bodywork.

Above left: Also red, also at Dunoon in May 1985, but this Leyland Leopard PSU4A/2R with Willowbrook body is owned by Cowal Motor Services. It was new in 1971 to Maidstone & District.

Left: From the late 1970s McGill's of Barrhead moved from double-deckers to Leyland Nationals. Most were bought new, but this 1979 10351A/1R model came from Strathclyde PTE in 1986. It is seen at Paisley Cross in March 1988.

Above: Seen on the island of Mull, *en route* from Craignure to Fionnphort, where passengers will catch the ferry to Iona, a 1978 Bedford YMT with Duple Dominant II bodywork in the fleet of Bowman, Craignure.

Left: The Rennie's of Dunfermline fleet trebled in size during the 1980s as the company became more heavily involved in contract and service work. For a period it competed with Fife Scottish in the Dunfermline area; this former London Transport Scania BR111DH/MCW Metropolitan was operating on a competitive service in Dunfermline in October 1987.

Right: Although Stagecoach had bought new double-deck coaches, it was 1989 before it bought new double-deck buses — Leyland Olympians with Alexander bodies. Outside the Falkirk coachworks of Walter Alexander in April 1989 is the Magic Bus 'Megadekka', billed as Britain's Biggest Bus. It is an Olympian ON6LXCT/5RZ with RL-type bodywork with 3+2 seating for an amazing 110 (66/44) passengers — hence the registration number. It was used first on services and contracts in the Glasgow area but was subsequently moved to various points within the Stagecoach fold. In 1988 Stagecoach had adopted this corporate livery for all of the vehicles in its growing empire.

77

Left: Keenan of Coalhall operated local services for a time around Ayr in competition with Western Scottish. Turning from the High Street into New Bridge Street, Ayr, is the former London Transport DM920, a 1974 Daimler Fleetline CRL6 with Park Royal bodywork.

Above: Although many smaller independents relied on second-hand acquisitions, others used new minibuses from dealer stock, like this 1989 Mercedes-Benz 811D with Alexander AM-type bodywork of McKenna of Uddingston, seen in Bellshill in June 1989.

Left: The bus-preservation movement in Scotland matured in the 1980s, largely as a result of the efforts of the Scottish Vintage Bus Museum. Lined up at its open day at Whitburn in August 1988 is a fine selection of preserved Scottish buses — from the right Glasgow Corporation L163 (1958 Leyland Titan PD2/24/Alexander), Scottish Omnibuses AA620 (1957 Bristol Lodekka LD6G/ECW), Alexanders RB161 (1953 Leyland Titan PD2/12/ Alexander), SMT J66 (1942 Leyland Titan TD5/ Alexander), Alexanders RO607 (1948 Guy Arab III/ Cravens) and Edinburgh Corporation 314 (1943 Guy Arab/1953 Duple/Nudd).

Below left: Glasgow's Museum of Transport re-opened in 1988 in part of the former Kelvin Hall exhibition area. It houses a fine selection of Glasgow trams as well as three buses. On the right is the final 'Cunarder' tramcar, No 1392 of 1952, while on the left can be seen three preserved Glasgow buses — 1949 Albion CX37S/Croft B92, 1958 BUT RETB1/Burlingham TBS13 and 1958 Leyland Atlantean PDR1/1/Alexander LA1.

Back cover: Perhaps more typical of modern Scotland than the front cover photograph, the new town of Glenrothes in Fife and Fife Scottish FRN4N, a 1973 Leyland Atlantean AN68/1R with Alexander AL-type body, photographed in October 1987. The bus was new to Aberdeen Corporation and passed to Fife via the corporation's successor, Grampian Regional Transport, introducing a new type to the Fife fleet.